Stories From Our House

Written by Richard Tulloch
Illustrated by Julie Vivas

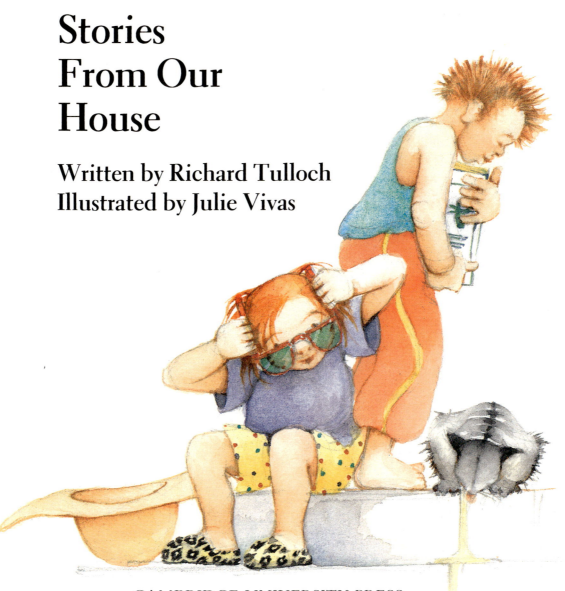

CAMBRIDGE UNIVERSITY PRESS
Cambridge
London New York New Rochelle
Melbourne Sydney

The Dog Next Door

Next door to our house there's a dog we like to play with.
He doesn't bite. He just licks you.
But he's a bad dog.

The dog next door knocked the lid off the bin outside our house. He pulled out some papers and cans. He pulled out some chicken bones and empty milk cartons and made a big mess all along the street. The smell was terrible.

The dog next door came into our garden and pulled the washing off our line. He tried to put my shirt on and he tore a hole in it.

When Mum saw what the dog next door had done, she was very angry.

'That dog should be locked up,' she said.

So Mum went to see the lady next door who owned the bad dog.

'It's about your dog,' said Mum. 'He knocked the lid off our bin and pulled the washing off our line. That dog should be locked up.'

'Oh, I am sorry,' said the lady next door.

And she locked the dog next door in her garage.

All day we could hear him scratching and whining, wanting to be let out. You could just see the tip of his wet nose under the garage door.

And at night he howled.

So Mum went to see the lady next door again.

'It's about your dog,' said Mum. 'It seems cruel to keep him locked up all day. If you let him out, I'll put a brick on top of my bin so he can't knock the lid off.'

'Thank you,' said the lady next door. 'I'm sure my dog would like to be let out.'

'And I'll keep our front gate shut,' said Mum, 'so he can't get in to tear up our washing.'

So the lady next door opened the garage . . .

. . . and out came the dog next door.

He was so happy.

He was so happy he jumped up and down, barking and wagging his tail.

He was so happy he knocked our bin right over, brick and all.

He was so happy he jumped right over our front gate and pulled down our washing line and tried to eat our socks.

The dog next door is a bad dog, but we like to play with him.

He doesn't bite. He just licks you.

The Ants

The ants came into our house, marching in a line.

A long brown line of ants, some of them coming and some of them going.

Under the door, across the wall and along the table in the kitchen.

Until they found a jar of honey.

They climbed up the side of the jar and ran round the edge and got their feet stuck in the gluey gooey honey.

Yuk!

Mum threw the honey jar out. She took a wet dishcloth and wiped up the ants. Then she turned on the tap and washed them down the sink.

But the next morning . . .

. . . the ants came back into our house, marching in a line.

A long brown line of ants, some of them coming and some of them going. Under the door, down the passage and out on to the porch.

Until they found a saucer of milk and cat food.

They crawled across the saucer and all over the cat food and some of them went for a swim in the milk.

Yuk!

Mum washed the saucer under the tap. She swept the ants off the porch with a stiff straw broom. She sucked the ants out of the passage with the vacuum cleaner.

But the next morning . . .

. . . the ants came back into our house, marching in a line.

A long brown line of ants, some of them coming and some of them going. Under the door, across the floor and up the leg of the table in the dining room.

Until they found a piece of cake with chocolate icing.

They pulled little crumbs from the cake and scattered them all over the floor.

One very greedy ant carried off a piece of chocolate icing three times as big as himself.

Mum threw the cake in the bin. Then she took a spray can and sprayed the line of ants.

Psssss! Pssssss!

We didn't like the smell. The ants didn't like it either. They ran round and round in circles. The greedy one dropped his chocolate icing.

Lots of them died, curled up on the shiny wet floor.

'I feel sorry for the ants, Mum,' I said.

'I feel sorry for them too,' said Mum, 'but I wish they wouldn't come marching through our house all the time. I don't know where they come from.'

So we followed the line of ants outside to see where they came from. Under the back door, across the yard, and round the corner of the house went the long brown line.

And there, between two bricks, was a little hole with a pile of sand round it.

And that's where the ants were coming from.

So now every day we leave some food close to the ants' house. Sometimes we leave honey and sometimes milk and cat food and sometimes a little piece of cake with chocolate icing.

The ants like the food, so they stay around their own house. But if ever we forget to feed them . . .

. . . the ants come back into our house, marching in a long brown line.

Some of them coming and some of them going, looking for something to eat.

Four Glass Drinking Mugs

We had four glass drinking mugs at our house.

Four glass mugs with handles.

Four glass mugs exactly the same.

We used our mugs at breakfast, four of us drinking milk and orange juice.

Then one day our baby was in a bad mood. He very accidentally threw his bowl of corn flakes right across the table.

'Look out!' we called.

'Catch it!' called Mum.

CRASH! went one glass drinking mug.

Then we had three glass drinking mugs.

Three glass mugs with handles.

Three glass mugs exactly the same.

We used our mugs when we sat outside on hot days. Three people drinking lemonade.

Then one day we were playing with a ball. We very accidentally threw the ball high up into the air.

It bounced on the wall, it bounced on the ground, it bounced on the table . . .

'Look out!' we called.

'Catch it!' called Mum.

CRASH! went another glass drinking mug.

Then we had two glass drinking mugs.

Two glass mugs with handles.

Two glass mugs exactly the same.

Mum and I used our mugs when we were working in the garden. I drank milk and she drank beer.

Mum put her mug on the fence post when she was raking up. The handle of the spade very accidentally knocked the fence . . .

'Look out!' I called.

'Catch it!' called Mum.

CRASH! went the glass drinking mug when it very accidentally hit a brick.

There was just one glass drinking mug left.
I looked after it for a long time.
I always held it very carefully.

Then one day . . .

. . . I slipped.

But a few days later Mum came in with a box.

'I've got a surprise!' she called.

In the box were four sparkling brand-new glass drinking mugs.

Four glass mugs with handles.

Four glass mugs exactly the same.

We all crowded round to look.

Our cat wanted to look too. He very accidentally jumped up on the table and bumped the four glass drinking mugs right over the edge . . .

'Look out!' we called.

'Catch them!' called Mum.

But the glass drinking mugs didn't break.

They were made of plastic.

Milk Trouble

In our house we've got milk trouble.

First our baby cries for his bottle.

Then Mum calls, 'Could someone please look after that baby while I put his milk on?'

And while we play with the baby, Mum puts the milk in the saucepan and puts the saucepan on the stove.

And that's when the milk trouble starts.

Then the telephone rings and Mum goes to answer it and says, 'Hello . . . oh no, I wasn't busy. I was just going to give the baby his bottle . . .'

And then she gets talking . . .

The milk bubbles up and boils up, out of the saucepan and on to the stove and down along the floor.

Sssssssttttttt!

And while we play with the baby, Mum cleans up the mess. There's always a mess with milk trouble.

And sometimes the trouble happens like this.

First our baby cries for his bottle.

Then Mum calls, 'Could someone please look after that baby while I put his milk on?'

And while we play with the baby, Mum puts the milk in a saucepan and puts the saucepan on the stove.

And that's when the milk trouble starts.

Then the doorbell rings and we call, 'Mum!' and she goes to the door and sees who it is and says, 'Hello, come through to the kitchen. I was just about to give the baby his bottle . . .'

And then she gets talking . . .

The milk bubbles up and boils up, out of the saucepan and on to the stove and down along the floor.

Sssssssstttttttt!

And while we play with the baby, Mum cleans up the mess. There's always a mess with milk trouble.

And Mum says, 'I don't think we'll ever get over this milk trouble.'

But we will.

When our baby gets bigger he'll drink cold milk from a glass.

Like we do.

The End

For Telma and Bram and Ana and Kate and those who clean up after them.

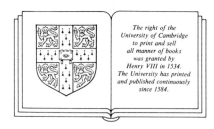

The right of the
University of Cambridge
to print and sell
all manner of books
was granted by
Henry VIII in 1534.
The University has printed
and published continuously
since 1584.

Published by the Press Syndicate of the University of Cambridge
The Pitt Building, Trumpington Street, Cambridge CB2 1RP
32 East 57th Street, New York, NY 10022, USA
10 Stamford Road, Oakleigh, Melbourne 3166, Australia

© Cambridge University Press 1987

First published 1987

Printed in Hong Kong by Wing King Tong

British Library cataloguing in publication data
Tulloch, Richard
Stories from our house.
I. Title II. Vivas, Julie
823'.914[J]   PZ7

Library of Congress cataloging in publication data
Tulloch, Richard.
Stories from our house.
Contents: The dog next door – The ants – Four glass drinking mugs – [etc.]
1. Children's stories, English. [1. Family life Fiction. 2. Humorous stories. 3. Short stories]
I. Vivas, Julie, 1947 – ill. II. Title.
PZ7.T82315St 1986 [E] 86-28370

ISBN 0 521 33485 3

CHOCTAW

Heather Bruegl

21st Century Junior Library

Indigenous Peoples of North America

Published in the United States of America by:

Cherry Lake Press
2395 South Huron Parkway, Suite 200, Ann Arbor, Michigan 48104
www.cherrylakepress.com

Reading Adviser: Beth Walker Gambro, MS, Ed., Reading Consultant, Yorkville, IL

Photo Credits: © Katie Hadley Photography, cover, title page; © Moab Republic/Shutterstock, 5; © AP Photo/The Oklahoman, Jaconna Aguirre, 6; © AP Photo/Rogelio V. Solis, 9; © wjarek/Shutterstock, 11; NASA image enhanced by BobNoah/Shutterstock, 13; © TLF Images/Shutterstock, 14; © AP Photo/Alonzo Adams File, 17; US Department of Agriculture via Flickr, 19; © David Creedon/Alamy Stock Photo, 21

Copyright © 2025 by Cherry Lake Publishing Group

All rights reserved. No part of this book may be reproduced or utilized in any form or by any means without written permission from the publisher.

Cherry Lake Press is an imprint of Cherry Lake Publishing Group.

Library of Congress Cataloging-in-Publication Data has been filed and is available at catalog.loc.gov.

Cherry Lake Publishing would like to acknowledge the work of the Partnership for 21st Century Learning, a network of Battelle for Kids. Please visit Battelle for Kids online for more information.

Printed in the United States of America

Note from publisher: Websites change regularly, and their future contents are outside of our control. Supervise children when conducting any recommended online searches for extended learning opportunities.

About the Cover: Beckah Boykin of Choctaw Nation served as consultant and model for a feature in *Brides of Oklahoma* (now Wed Society Oklahoma) magazine called "A Vibrant Tradition: A Walk Through the Choctaw Wedding Aesthetic." The feature produced the image shown on the cover as well as others that highlight Choctaw wedding traditions. Boykin works as a model and actress. She is also a Choctaw social dancer, hymn artist, and stickball player.

CONTENTS

Who We Are	4
Our Lives Today	10
Our Ancestral Lands	15
Carrying Traditions Forward	18
Glossary	22
Find Out More	23
Index	24
About the Author	24

WHO WE ARE

The Choctaw people call themselves *Chahta*. They are an Indigenous group. The land that is now the United States has been their home for thousands of years. The Choctaw people value faith, family, and culture. They recognize a deep connection among all living things. As with many Indigenous groups, Choctaw elders help preserve culture and knowledge. The Choctaw use this knowledge to grow and prosper.

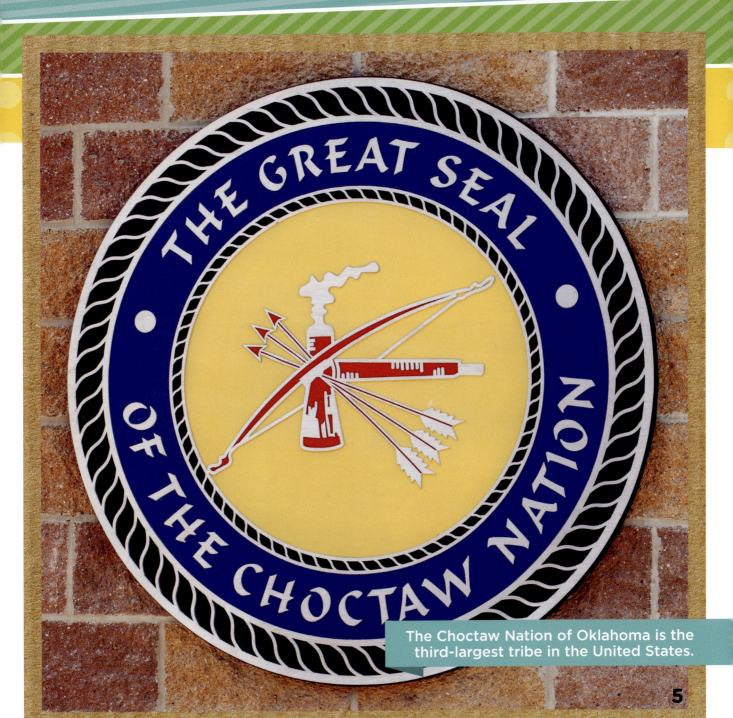
The Choctaw Nation of Oklahoma is the third-largest tribe in the United States.

The Choctaw language is an important part of Choctaw life. It is important to Choctaw identity. The language keeps them connected to their ancestors. It helps them connect with future generations.

The Choctaw language was first written down just a few hundred years ago. It uses a version of the Latin alphabet like English does.

Think!
What does being a good neighbor mean to you? How can you work to be a good neighbor in your life?

Choctaw values also include being a good neighbor. Through fairness and service, the Choctaw believe in strength through togetherness.

Choctaw culture grows and changes. It builds on past traditions. For example, stickball is a popular Choctaw sport. Traditionally, it helped settle arguments between families. Today, the World Series of Stickball is a championship tournament. The sport might even help settle arguments between nations.

Choctaw basket making, pottery, storytelling, art, and dance are all traditions that thrive today. The skills and art forms are passed down from generation to generation. Each artist combines modern ideas with traditional methods. This adds layers to the rich and vibrant Choctaw culture. It is a culture that is very much alive today.

There are three **federally recognized** Choctaw bands. These are the Choctaw Nation of Oklahoma, the Mississippi Band of Choctaw Indians, and the Jena Band of Choctaw Indians in Louisiana. Each band shares a common culture and language, but each has its own history and government.

Look!

Look at the picture of a Choctaw stickball game. Why do you think it is called stickball? What other sports does it remind you of?

OUR LIVES TODAY

Today, most Choctaw people live in Oklahoma and Mississippi. Each of the three Choctaw tribal nations has its own **reservation**. The largest is in southeastern Oklahoma. It is home to the Choctaw Nation of Oklahoma. It is around 11,000 square miles (28,490 square kilometers). Many Choctaw also live on the Mississippi and Louisiana reservations.

Choctaw people are an important part of American life. They contribute to many fields, including the arts and sciences.

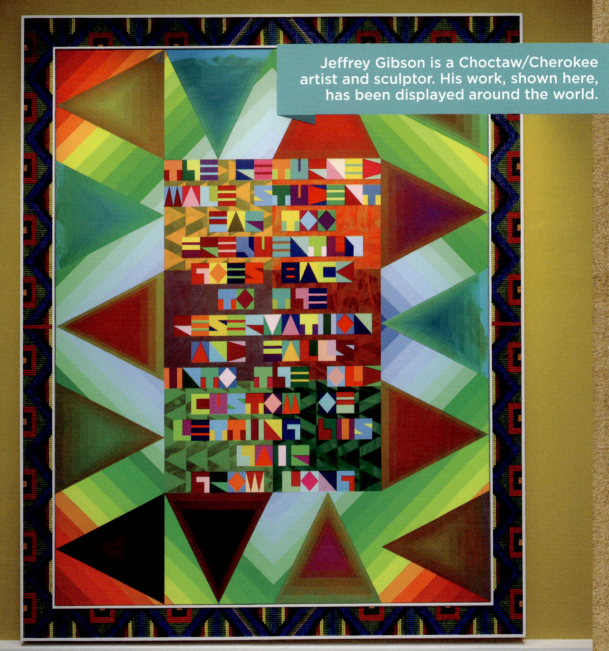

Jeffrey Gibson is a Choctaw/Cherokee artist and sculptor. His work, shown here, has been displayed around the world.

In 2023, **heirloom** Choctaw seeds traveled to space! These seeds were saved for generations. They were sewn into clothes. This kept them safe on long journeys. These seeds represent America's oldest crops. Scientists will study how these seeds grow in space.

Choctaw sacred lands in Mississippi are still important. One such place is the Choctaw Mother Mound. It is called *Nanih Waiya* or the "slanted mound." Choctaw tradition says this is where the Choctaw began. This land was lost in a treaty with the United States. But in 2008, this sacred land was returned to the Mississippi Band of Choctaw.

Choctaw seeds on the International Space Station

Create!

Research ancient mounds in Mississippi and Alabama. Choose three. Create a travel brochure with facts and images that guide visitors along a route to visit all three.

Choctaw communities thrived in these lands for generations, and some still do today.

OUR ANCESTRAL LANDS

The Choctaw people originally called the southeastern United States home. Their lands covered parts of Mississippi, Louisiana, and Alabama. The land was rich and **fertile**. The Choctaw were expert farmers. They farmed in the **Three Sisters** method. They planted corn, beans, and squash. They grew other crops such as sunflowers. They also gathered berries and other edible wild plants. They sometimes grew more than they needed. They traded extra crops with neighboring tribes.

The Choctaw took great care of the land. They used controlled burns. This is a type of **forest management**. It helps clear land for new plants. It can also help keep the soil fertile. Along with other Indigenous nations, the Choctaw view the land as a living and breathing being. It is something that must be preserved for future generations.

In 1830, the U.S. Congress passed the **Indian Removal Act**. The Choctaw were forced to leave their homelands. If they didn't, the United States

Make a Guess!

Why do you think the Three Sisters are such important crops? If you said it is because of the complete nutrition they provide, you'd be right!

Gary Batton is the 47th chief of the Choctaw Nation. Choctaw leaders today help defend land and water rights.

threatened to destroy them. The Choctaw signed a removal treaty. This meant they had to rebuild their lives in **Indian Territory**. That land is part of Oklahoma today. Not all Choctaw left. Some still live on their ancestral lands. Those that did leave faced a hard journey. One-third to one-fourth of Choctaw people died. The Choctaw Trail of Tears was a time of great sorrow.

CARRYING TRADITIONS FORWARD

Choctaw people still remember and honor those lost during removal. Each year, they hold a Trail of Tears Memorial Walk. They remember the journey. They also celebrate how much survivors overcame. Those who survived set up new governments. They built schools. They built farms. The Choctaw Nation became the strongest economy in Indian Territory.

Ask Questions!

What questions do you have about how Choctaw people adapted to change? Find a librarian, teacher, or adult to help you find answers to your questions.

The Choctaw way of life continued. Their spirit of generosity was not defeated. In 1847, the Choctaw learned of the **Great Hunger** in Ireland. People there were starving. The Choctaw raised what would be $5,000 in today's U.S. dollars. They sent it to the town of Midleton. That is in County Cork, Ireland. The Irish learned the money came from the Choctaw many years later. The Irish people have a history of **colonization**, too. Their appreciation brought the two peoples together in friendship.

The relationship between the Irish and the Choctaw continues today. It includes scholarships to send Choctaw students to study in Ireland. When the

COVID-19 pandemic started, the Irish organized a fundraising event. They sent the money raised to support not only the Choctaw but also the Diné (Navajo) and Hopi peoples. These peoples were suffering. These donations were in honor of and in thanks for the help the Choctaw gave to the Irish.

This Kindred Spirits monument stands in County Cork, Ireland, in honor of the Choctaw Nation.

GLOSSARY

colonization (kah-luh-nuh-ZAY-shuhn) the act of settling in an area and exercising control over Indigenous peoples

federally recognized (FEH-druh-lee REH-kig-niezd) a status assigned to U.S. tribal nations by the federal government that provides specific rights and benefits

fertile (FUHR-tuhl) full of nutrients and able to support growth

forest management (FOR-uhst MA-nij-muhnt) the act of taking care of forests and wild spaces to encourage growth and health

Great Hunger (GRAYT HUN-guhr) commonly called the Irish Potato Famine; a time in Ireland of great starvation and disease from 1845 to 1852

heirloom (AIR-loom) a plant variety that is unchanged over several generations

Indian Removal Act (IN-dee-uhn rih-MOO-vuhl AKT) a law passed in 1830 that moved tribes living in the southeastern part of the United States to west of the Mississippi

Indian Territory (IN-dee-uhn TAIR-uh-tor-ee) the U.S. area west of the Mississippi River where Indigenous peoples were forced to move; today is the state of Oklahoma

reservation (reh-zuhr-VAY-shuhn) a legally designated plot of land held in trust for Indigenous peoples by the U.S. federal government

Three Sisters (THREE SIH-sterz) a form of planting in Indigenous communities that refers to the planting of corn, beans, and squash

FIND OUT MORE

Books
Bruegl, Heather. *Indian Removal*. Ann Arbor, MI: Cherry Lake Press, 2024.

Sorell, Traci. *We Are Grateful: Otsaliheliga*. Watertown, MA: Charlesbridge, 2021.

Sorell, Traci. *We Are Still Here! Native American Truths Everyone Should Know*. Watertown, MA: Charlesbridge, 2021.

Online
With an adult, explore more online with these suggested searches.

- MBCI World Series Stickball via YouTube
- "School of Language Resources," Choctaw Nation of Oklahoma

Say Hello!
Halito (huh-lee-TOE) is a way to say "hi" in Choctaw.

INDEX

agriculture, 12, 15–16
art and artists, 8, 11, 19, 21

Batton, Gary, 17

Choctaw Nation of Oklahoma, 8, 10, 17, 18
Choctaw people, 4–9, 10–12, 14–21
   language, 6
   modern life, 10–13, 18–21
   photographs, 6, 9, 17
civil and land rights, 15–16
colonialism, 16–17, 20
cultural preservation, 4, 6–9, 12, 18

environmental values, 16

forced migration, 15–16, 18

generosity, 20–21
Gibson, Jeffrey, 11

Indian Removal Act (1830), 15–16
Irish-Choctaw relations, 20–21

Jena Band of Choctaw Indians (Louisiana), 8, 10

lands, 4, 10, 12, 14–17
language, 6

Mississippi Band of Choctaw, 8, 10, 12
mounds, 12, 13

Oklahoma, 17

population areas, 8, 10

reservations, 10

Southern United States, 8, 10, 12, 13, 14–17
stickball, 7, 9

traditions, preservation, 4, 6–9, 12
Trail of Tears, 17, 18

U.S. government, 15–16

ABOUT THE AUTHOR

Heather Bruegl, a member of the Oneida Nation of Wisconsin/Stockbridge-Munsee, is a Madonna University graduate with a Master of Arts in U.S. History. She is a public historian and decolonial educator, and her Munsee name is Kiishookunkwe, which means "Sunflower in Full Bloom." Heather frequently travels to present on Indigenous history, policy, and activism, bringing her deep knowledge and personal connection to the subject.